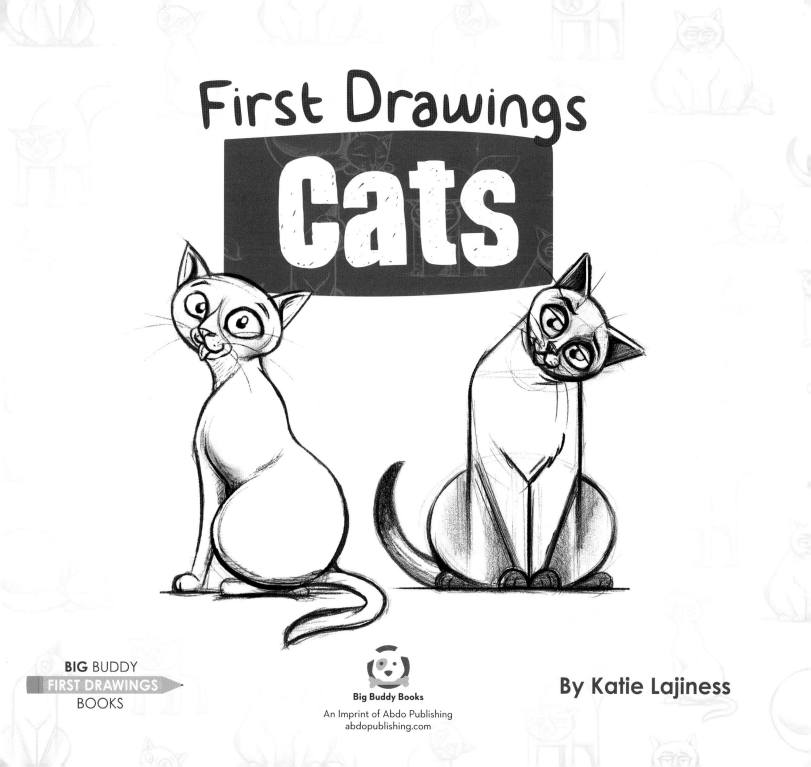

# First Drawings
# Cats

BIG BUDDY
FIRST DRAWINGS
BOOKS

Big Buddy Books
An Imprint of Abdo Publishing
abdopublishing.com

By Katie Lajiness

**abdopublishing.com**

Published by Abdo Publishing, a division of ABDO, PO Box 398166, Minneapolis, Minnesota 55439.
Copyright © 2017 by Abdo Consulting Group, Inc. International copyrights reserved in all countries. No part
of this book may be reproduced in any form without written permission from the publisher. Big Buddy Books™
is a trademark and logo of Abdo Publishing.

Printed in the United States of America, North Mankato, Minnesota.
092016
012017

THIS BOOK CONTAINS
RECYCLED MATERIALS

Illustrations: Michael Jacobsen/Spectrum Studio
Interior Photos: Deposit Photos

Coordinating Series Editor: Tamara L. Britton
Graphic Design: Taylor Higgins, Maria Hosley


**Publisher's Cataloging-in-Publication Data**

Names: Lajiness, Katie, author.
Title: Cats / by Katie Lajiness.
Description: Minneapolis, MN : Abdo Publishing, 2017. | Series: First drawings |
    Includes index.
Identifiers: LCCN 2016945189 | ISBN 9781680785210 (lib. bdg.) |
    ISBN 9781680798814 (ebook)
Subjects:  LCSH: Cats in art--Juvenile literature. | Drawing--Technique--Juvenile
    literature.
Classification: DDC 743.6/9752--dc23
LC record available at http://lccn.loc.gov/2016945189

# Table of Contents

# Getting Started

Today, you're going to draw cats. Not sure you know how to draw? Cats are easy to **sketch** if you break them down into circles, ovals, rectangles, squares, and triangles.

To begin, you'll need paper, a sharpened pencil, a big eraser, and a flat surface. Draw each shape lightly. When these **guidelines** are light, it is easy to erase and try again.

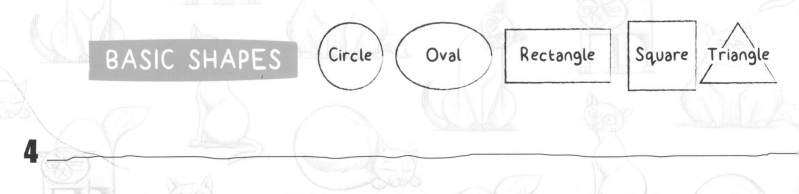

BASIC SHAPES — Circle, Oval, Rectangle, Square, Triangle

Goofy Cat

Sleepy Cat

Crabby Cat

Fat Cat

Curious Cat

# Adding Color

Once you learn to draw an object, you may want to add color. Let's learn how to mix colors and add shading.

## Shading

**MARKERS**
Use similar colors to create shading.

**PENCILS AND CRAYONS**
Use less pressure for lighter shades and more pressure for darker shades.

**PAINTS**
Add white to lighten and black or blue to darken shades.

There are three primary colors. They are red, yellow, and blue. These colors cannot be made by mixing other colors. However, you can make many colors by mixing primary colors together.

Color mixing

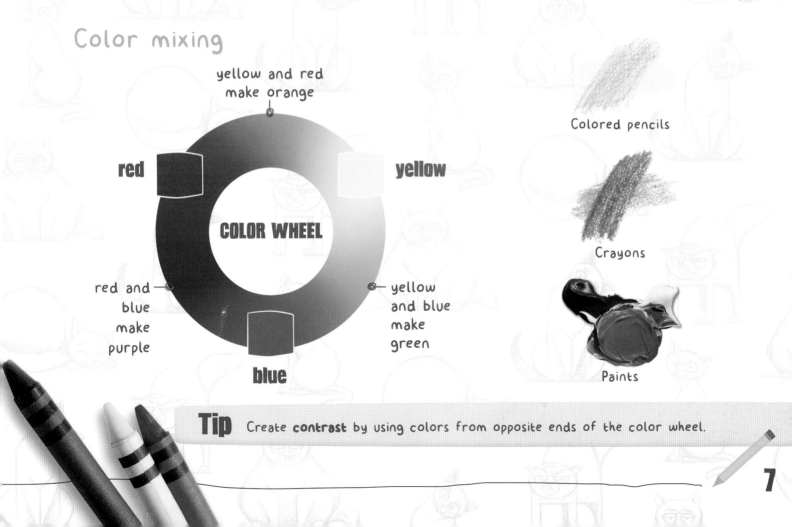

yellow and red
make orange

red

COLOR WHEEL

yellow

red and
blue
make
purple

yellow
and blue
make
green

blue

Colored pencils

Crayons

Paints

Tip  Create **contrast** by using colors from opposite ends of the color wheel.

# Goofy Cat

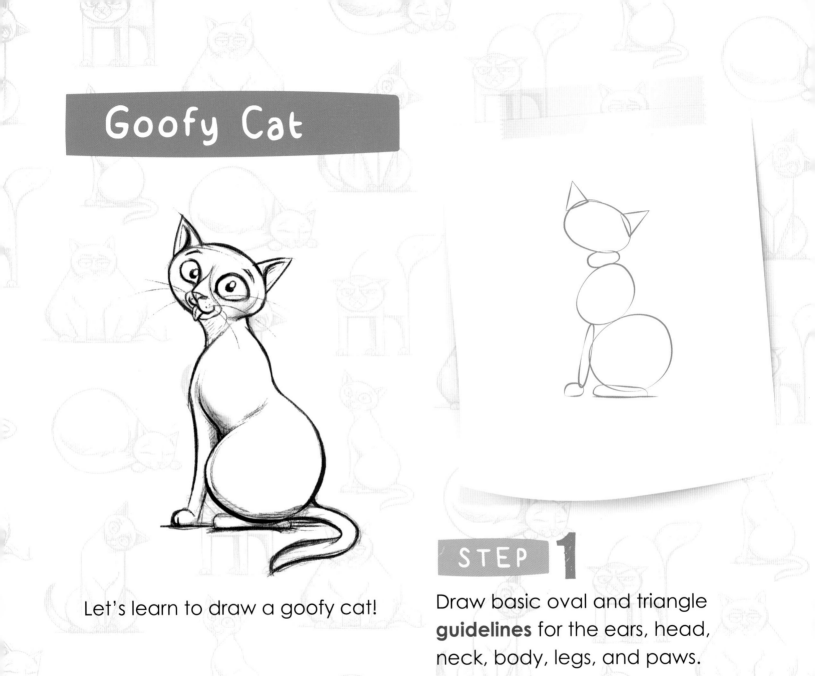

Let's learn to draw a goofy cat!

Draw basic oval and triangle **guidelines** for the ears, head, neck, body, legs, and paws.

Erase guidelines
once you have
the parts drawn.

Connect the shapes to form
the cat's **outline**.

Add a tail. Draw a line to show
**detail** in the paw. **Sketch guidelines**
across the cat's face.

9

Erase guidelines once you have the parts drawn.

Add large eyes, nose, and a loopy W for the mouth.

Include **details** such as pupils, eyebrows, whiskers, and a tongue. Create **texture** and shape by shading your goofy cat.

Bravo! You drew
a goofy cat.

STEP 6

It's time for some color! You can
add your own color and shading
to personalize your drawing.

# Sleepy Cat

Let's learn to draw a sleepy cat!

Draw basic triangle and circle **guidelines** for the ears, head, and body.

Erase guidelines once you have the parts drawn.

Connect the shapes to form the cat's **outline**.

Add body features such as a tail and paws. **Sketch** light **guidelines** across the cat's face.

Erase guidelines
once you have
the parts drawn.

## STEP 4

Draw closed eyes, eyebrows, a nose, and a loopy *W* for the mouth. Make the tail fluffy by adding fur.

## STEP 5

Add **details** to the paws. Draw in whiskers. Create **texture** and shape by adding shading to your sleepy cat.

It's time for some color! You can add your own color and shading to personalize your drawing.

Well done! You drew a sleepy cat.

# Crabby Cat

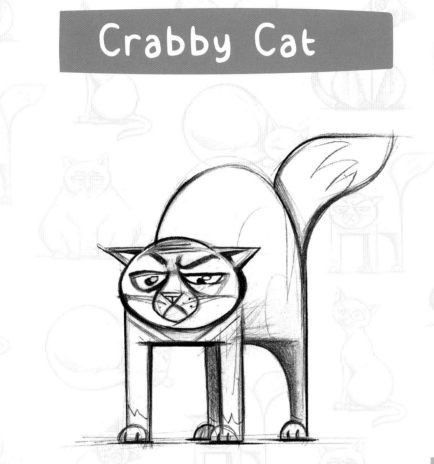

Let's learn to draw a crabby cat!

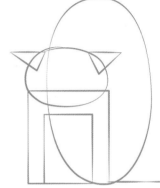

Draw basic oval, triangle, and rectangle **guidelines** for the head, ears, body, and legs.

Erase guidelines once you have the parts drawn.

Connect the shapes to form the cat's **outline**.

Add body features such as a tail and paws. **Sketch** light **guidelines** across the cat's face.

Erase guidelines once you have the parts drawn.

# STEP 4

Add narrow eyes, eyebrows, a nose, and a frown for the mouth. Create a *U* around the nose and mouth for the muzzle.

# STEP 5

Draw in the pupils and whiskers. Add **details** to the paws. Create **texture** and shape by adding shading to your cat.

It's time to add some color! You can add your own color and shading to personalize your drawing.

**YOU DID IT!**

Congratulations! You drew a crabby cat.

Let's learn to draw a fat cat!

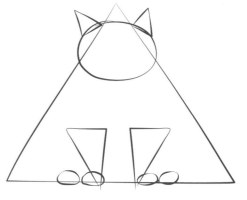

## STEP 1

Draw basic triangle and circle **guidelines** for the ears, head, body, legs, and paws.

Erase guidelines once you
have the parts drawn.

STEP **2**

Connect the shapes to form
the cat's **outline**.

STEP **3**

Add body features such as a tail
and fur. Draw **guidelines** across
your cat's face.

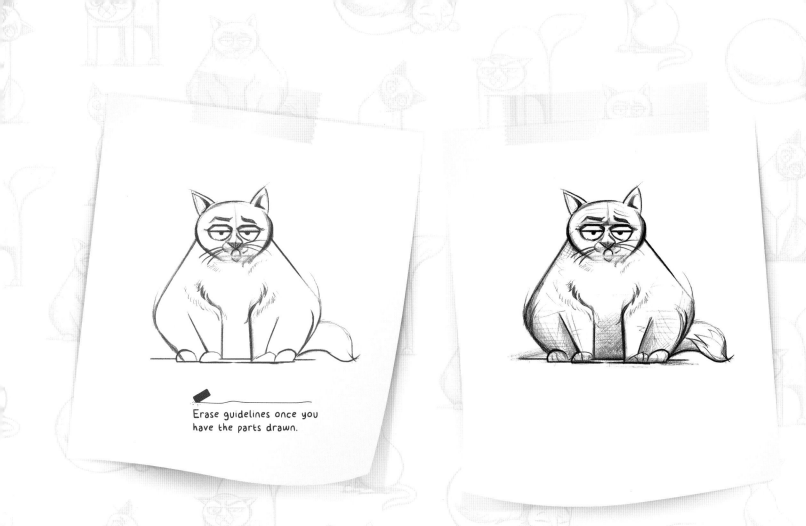

Erase guidelines once you have the parts drawn.

STEP **4**

Draw half-closed eyes, eyebrows, a nose, and a frown for the mouth. Add whiskers and fur **details** to face.

STEP **5**

Add details to the paws. Create **texture** and shape by adding shading to your cat.

## STEP 6

It's time for some color! You can add your own color and shading to personalize your drawing.

Yippee! You drew a fat cat.

23

# Curious Cat

Let's learn to draw a curious cat!

## STEP 1

Draw basic triangle, oval, and rectangle **guidelines** for the ears, head, and body.

Erase guidelines
once you have
the parts drawn.

# STEP 2

Connect the shapes to form the cat's **outline**.

# STEP 3

Use two triangle **guidelines** to help shape the front legs.

Erase guidelines once you have the parts drawn.

## STEP 4

**Sketch** in the front legs to create **depth**.

## STEP 5

Add paws and draw a tail for your cat.

Erase guidelines once you have the parts drawn.

# STEP 6

**Sketch guidelines** across the cat's face.

# STEP 7

Add large eyes, eyebrows, and a loopy *W* for the mouth.

Fill in the eyes and add whiskers to finish your cat's face.

Add **details** to the paws. Create **texture** and shape by adding shading.

**Tools** There are many tools you can use to add color such as crayons, colored pencils, paints, or markers.

It's time for some color! You can add your own color and shading to personalize your drawing.

YOU DID IT!

Yay! You drew a curious cat.

To build your drawing skills, practice finding basic shapes in everyday objects. Finding basic shapes can help you draw almost anything. Use what you've learned to draw other cats. The more you draw, the better you will be!

# Glossary

**contrast** the amount of difference in color or brightness.

**depth** measurement from top to bottom or from front to back.

**detail** a minor decoration, such as a cat's whiskers.

**guideline** a rule or instruction that shows or tells how something should be done.

**outline** the outer edges of a shape.

**sketch** to make a rough drawing.

**texture** the look or feel of something.

# Websites

To learn more about First Drawings, visit **booklinks.abdopublishing.com**. These links are routinely monitored and updated to provide the most current information available.

# Index